Practicing Death

Make the Most Out of Your Life

Ranan Lachman

First Published in United States of America in 2020 by
Stonehome Press Publishing

Copyright © 2020 by Ranan Lachman

The right of Ranan Lachman to be identified as the Author of the Work has been Asserted by him in accordance with the Copyright, Designs and
Patents Act 1988.

All rights reserved. No part of this publication may be reproduced, stored in a retrieval system, or transmitted, in any form or by any means without the prior written permission of the publisher, nor be otherwise circulated in any form of binding or cover other than that in which it is published and without a similar condition being imposed on the subsequent purchaser.

ISBN: 978-1-5136-5459-1

Typeset in Minion Pro by Clark Kenyon

Stonehome Press books may be purchased for education, business, or sales promotional use. For more information please email sales@stonehomepress.com

Library of Congress Control Number: 2016904683

Dedicated to my beloved wife, Michelle, who continues to support my death practice (even if wishing, sometimes, that I'll achieve mastery...)

ABOUT THE AUTHOR

Few years ago, my sister, who i'm very close to, was diagnosed with late-stage breast cancer while nursing her four month old baby. Going through a torturous year of medical treatments and managing through this near-death experience transformed my views on life.

It created a sense of urgency to focus on purposeful activities and dedicate substantial time to the people I love – all, before it's too late. With this new insight, I quit the nine-to-five work office setting, sold our belongings, and together with my wife and two children decided to accomplish a lifelong dream: travel around the world for a year. We drove a motor home from California to Chile for 10 months, and then continued to Asia.

Practicing Death was developed as a result of this unique experience; realizing that the greatest transformations in people's lives usually follow a near-death experience (such as a heart attack, car accident or cancer). Consequently, if one can simulate their death, they could gain all the benefits of profound realizations without the physical risk.

Eureka!

The straight-forward death-simulation practice, described in this book, takes only 10 minutes a week. It helps readers to prioritize their time, reduces their anxiety and fear of death and provides a sense of urgency to take action.

Ranan Lachman is an accomplished business professional, triathlete and author. He lives in Bali with his wife and two young children.

More from the Author:
Now Available in book stores and on Amazon.com

CONTENTS

1. Why Practice Death? Becoming a Believer — 1
2. A Powerful Moment — 9
3. Live With the End in Mind — 15
4. The Fear of Death — 25
5. Benefits of Practicing Death — 37
6. Technique for Practicing Death — 51
7. Spirituality in Practicing Death — 65
8. What We Can Learn from Near-Death Experiences — 75
9. Final Thoughts — 103
   Appendix A — 105
   Appendix B — 110

CHAPTER 1

Why Practice Death? Becoming a Believer

"I'm not afraid to die I just don't want to be there when it happens."

—Woody Allen

Three years ago, when my sister, Keren was only thirty-nine years old, she was diagnosed with late-stage breast cancer. She realized there was a problem when her newly born baby abruptly stopped nursing from one of her mammery glands. The fear that her cancer already spread to other organs was real and waiting for the results of the operation that was scheduled to test if it indeed spread was especially excruciating. She had four young children under the age of five including a newborn and the thought of losing their mom at such an early age was devastating.

Everyone, on some level or another, knows they're going to die at some point. Yet like so many others, we were shocked that it is happening much sooner than we ever anticipated.

I had always tried to avoid thinking about death, as I hoped it would be something I would need to deal with only later in life—much, much later.

When the test results came back and showed the cancer had not spread, we were the happiest people on Earth. The immediate death sentence was temporarily removed and the oncologist informed us that if Keren went through a torturous year-long treatment that included chemo therapy, radiation, and then mastectomy, there was a decent change she'd survive cancer. Over the next year, Keren lost her hair, eyebrows, and some of her self-esteem, but at the end of the year-long treatment, she was declared cancer free and is on medications for the next ten years to help prevent its reoccurrence.

When people experience a near-death experience, something magical happens. The person experiencing it obtains a new realization about life—a clear, profound understanding of what they need to do to make the most of their remaining time on earth, now that they have been given a second chance.

> The greatest transformations in life happen to people that experienced a near-death event. Somehow they obtain a clear realization about life's priorities.

Keren told me, *"when I was initially diagnosed, my world collapsed in a second. I was only 39, very young to get any type of cancer, and with four little kids to take care of, I kept of asking, why me?. I felt betrayed by my body, and the world.*

Death was lurking around the corner and I was really feeling that this is the end of my life.

I went through a very painful mental process of overcoming grieving the loss of the life I still haven't lost. Grieving my femininity that will be impacted forever by the loss of my breast, a part of my body that was important for me.

I attended a support group that recommended me to read couple of books that literally changed my life forever. They saved my spirit from breaking and made me a stronger person. I'm now a more compassionate and empathetic to others and see my cancer as an amazing growth opportunity. I'm now grateful that I went through this experience as I'm a much better person now then I was before. I stareted to appreciate life's routine and the life that occurs around us every day. I don't take for granted the first breath I take every morning. Getting close to death allowed me to stop, open my eyes and get the perspective I needed to change my view point about life and the people around me. It was a hard process to go through and while I never wish to anyone to get cancer, the realization that comes with overcoming this harship while seeing your death nearby, is invaluable."

Chances are good you have a friend, family member, or a colleague who had a similar near-death experience. It's amazing that the greatest transformations in life happen after such an experience, when the person affected realizes that they almost lost their life. Now, that they are saved, they decide to focus their energy on more meaningful activities, with the people who truly matter for them, celebrating and honoring the miracle that they managed to survive.

As my sister's cancer treatment ended, my wife came to me with a crazy and transformational idea. She wanted us to change our boring suburban life, sell all our belongings, get the children out of school, leave California, and embark on a year-long trip around the world. She wanted to spend time with our kids and see the world, and there is nothing more bonding for a family than cramming us all into a small motor home and road-schooling the kids on the go. Crazy, right?

Crazy it is, but that's exactly what we decided to do!

We always dreamed about traveling around the world after we retired. But we realized that our days are numbered and waiting for retirement might be too late (and chances are good the children wouldn't want to join us then, anyway).

So, we dropped everything and for a year, we drove from California to Chile, over 23,000 miles in a motor home, and had an experience of a lifetime. We lived with each other 24/7 for 52 weeks in a space of 40 Square feet. We truly lived life every moment, saw new and exciting places, and collected precious memories as a family. We learned a new language, tasted incredible and eclectic food, formed relationships with many travelers along the way and even built with locals a bridge from river stones. The bridge collapsed during a three-day tropical storm we happen to run into and it was the only way out of the village we got stuck in, so we all worked together to rebuild it. We met fascinating people along the way and, most importantly, bonded as a family.

I never imagined wanting to be a teacher as I never had a patience for teaching young kids. Then suddenly for 10 months, I became the teacher of my kids which we road-schooled while driving the motorhome south to Chile. It was a new, exciting yet challenging experience. As my children preferred many times to play video games than do another math lesson it also tested me as a father. But the spark of excitement when they mastered a new topic and solved problems by themselves was invaluable and taught us that we can achieve new things together.

We also had to overcome many predisposed fears as we needed to stay overnight on the side of the road in many "dangerous" countries and areas with reputation for crime. We drove through cartel areas in Mexico, Honduras and Columbia and found only friendly people around us who were willing to help at any turn. We haven't seen or noticed any of the crime we were so afraid of.

And while we did experience one car break in, when our motorhome small windshield was broken into in Peru, mainly due to our fault as we parked it in a really bad spot, we used it as a learning opportunity of how to deal with such predicaments. In less than an hour we managed to replace the broken window with a makeshift window that was cut from a different brand car windshield and cost only $3.00 to cut and install.

As part of this trip, we also stumbled into Bali, Indonesia, a magical exotic island which we now call our home and from where I'm writing this book. Without a doubt, my sister's near-death experience led to wonderful transformation in our lives, which we are all truly thankful for.

If experiencing that proximity to death can cause such an amazing and positive transformation, leading people to change their lives for the better, the question that comes to mind is, *Why can't we simulate it?* Why can't we reap all the amazing benefits of obtaining clarity, focus, and changing our lives without putting ourselves at physical risk?

The answer is that we can!

> **If experiencing near-death creates positive transformation, why can't we simulate a safe death to reap all the benefits?**

This book will teach you a technique which, if practiced regularly for just ten minutes a week, can improve your life. You don't need to get closer to your actual death in order to gain the benefits people, who got closer to death, achieved.

Don't believe it? Just try the short exercise on the next page and chances are good, you'll become a believer!

CHAPTER 2

A Powerful Moment

"Awareness of death is the very bedrock of the path. Until you have developed this awareness, all other practices are useless."

—The Dalai Lama

Let's start with a short but very powerful exercise. Do not skip this exercise.

For the next minute, please don't look at your smartphone or get distracted—it will only take fifteen seconds!

If possible, find a quiet corner, get into an empty room, close the door, and sit on a chair comfortably. Hold nothing but this book.

When you are ready . . . turn the page, read the sentence on the next page, and close your eyes for fifteen seconds (no need to count, just guestimate).

Ready? Now, turn to the next page.

You are told by a trusted doctor that you are going to die in fifteen seconds.

Please close your eyes and prepare for your death.

After approximately twenty seconds, open your eyes, take a deep breath and try to calm your mind.

How do you feel? Are you calm? Angry? Frustrated that life was taken away from you without notice and that you weren't able to accomplish all the amazing things that you planned to achieve?

In the last year, I've conducted this exact same exercise on several hundred individuals. Their nationalities, ages, gender, and upbringings were all very different. Yet they all had a similar experience.

What happens to your mind during those fifteen seconds?

When you learned that in fifteen seconds, you were going to die, your mind focused. Everything was simplified, your daily troubles were vanished, as they were no longer relevant. What does any of it matter if you are going to die?

This is the power of death. It grabs your attention, filters out the clutter, and provides you with new realizations.

The vast majority of individuals I've conducted this exercise with experienced the same scene in their head. They became serene and calm, seeing themselves lying on a bed, surrounded by white light. They saw themselves from a higher vantage point, as if they were seeing themselves from the outside, surrounded by close family members and friends. These people hugged them gently in peace and serenity and then their body seemed to vanish into the light. At this point, they opened

> **Death grabs your attention, filters out the clutter, and provides you with new real zations.**

their eyes in astonishment, sometimes with tears in their eyes, sometimes with a shocked expression on their faces.

This exercise, if done with sincere intention and the proper conditions, can be very powerful and bring certain individuals to new transformational realizations after it is analyzed.

In the next chapter, you will gain a better understanding of why death is such a powerful catalyst for transformation.

CHAPTER 3

Live With the End in Mind

"In the end, it's not the years in your life that count. It's the life in your years."

—Abraham Lincoln

Picture this: You're driving to the supermarket to pick up some groceries. You're rushing, as you've promised your spouse to be back home in time for dinner. Suddenly, a truck on your left swerves to the right, hits the side of your car, and your vehicle slams into a telephone pole. Your head smashes into the wheel.

Silence.

Everything has stopped as you try to comprehend what just happened. You haul your eyelids up. While it seems vague, you start identifying people walking in the distance. Through the haze, you seem to recognize some of them and notice they're all dressed up in black. "How strange," you think to yourself.

As they walk quietly away from you toward what looks like

a chapel, your body seems to float toward them in an effort to catch up with the figures you now fully recognize as your friends and family. When you finally reach them, you extend your hand to touch a longtime pal's shoulder in the hopes of getting his attention. At that moment, you realize they are all here for a reason: they are standing around a coffin.

You peek behind your friend's shoulder to see who's being buried, and you're shocked to recognize *your* face in that coffin. They're gathered for your funeral!

You are stunned in disbelief, frozen when you notice your eldest son taking a few steps forward from the crowd. He pulls a note from his pocket and starts reading something; it's your eulogy. You're dumbfounded and want to shout for him to stop, yet no sound is coming out of your mouth. You wave your hands and push through the crowd, but no one seems to see you.

Unable to be seen or heard, you decide to listen to what people say about you. One after another they come to the little podium—your spouse, your best friend, and an office colleague whom you never really liked—and say their parting words.

What do they say about you? Did your life have any impact on them? Was your life worth living according to how you are remembered by the people who were closest to you? Could you have done better?

We are born knowing we'll die one day. Invariably, it always happens too soon, and while our mind knows that our life is finite, we reject the notion of our death on a daily basis.

We push death into a far corner of our brain, seeing it as a vague possibility, pushing it so deep that it never seems real. But it's real and it's something that will happen eventually. Yet, when it happens, it's too late to make adjustments to what we did or weren't able to do in life (and how you might be remembered as by others).

> Every day we reject the notion that we can die today, but it's always there...

In 2017, I surveyed 1,500 American adults between the ages of twenty and fifty, by asking them a basic question: *What do you wish for yourself?* The most common answers were:

1. I wish I had more money.
2. I wish to get a promotion.
3. I wish to own my home.
4. I wish I had more sex.
5. I wish to be famous.

The results for this survey shows that many in the western world live their life in pursuit of money, power, and sexual gratification. You, too, might relate to many of these same wishes.

Now, let's look at another survey[1] conducted by Bonnie Ware. Bonnie worked for twenty-seven years as a palliative care nurse in a hospital. In her work, she helped the seriously ill through their suffering and was there to hear the realizations during their final days. In her book, *The Top Five Regrets of the Dying*, she summarized what her patients expressed in their most sincere and sensitive final moments. The top five wishes of the dying were:

1. I wish I'd had the courage to live a life true to myself, not the life others expected of me.
2. I wish I hadn't worked so hard.
3. I wish I'd had the courage to express my feelings.
4. I wish I had stayed in touch with my friends.
5. I wish that I had let myself be happier.

Now compare the list of the five regrets of the dying with the wishes of the living. It is astonishing to realize that what we tend to wish for during our earlier years seem totally unimportant and meaningless when we look back at our life and prioritize what was REALLY important to us.

> Amazingly, the things we wish for during our lives seem meaningless in retrospect. On our death bed we tend to regret that we got our priorities wrong.

In the top regrets of the patients who were about to die, the words *money, career, possession, sex,* or *power* were never mentioned. When it comes to career, the paradox is even greater—while people seem to fixate on achieving promotions (which usually means they'll be required to work even harder with longer hours), they later will regret they dedicated so much time to their career.

What can we learn from this?

Why should we live a less satisfying life until it's too late to make a change? Why don't we learn from the wisdom of the millions of individuals who lived their life exactly as we are, but now, on their death bed, they know better and can provide us the key to a better life? Why don't we learn from their mistakes?

The answer is that, for most people, it is hard to learn from other peoples' experience. We can listen and understand, but it is very hard to truly absorb and make real changes in our own lives following someone else's advice. As humans, we tend to learn much better when we go through the experience ourselves. Only then does the experience becomes tangible and we are more open to act on it and make meaningful transformational changes to our lives.

That is why this book advocates the idea of practicing death. When we do so, we truly allow ourselves to gain the insights of our own wiser-selves and see our lives in perspective. Through this narrow lens we can eliminate the clutter of the daily and mundane and see clearly the things that are truly important to us.

It allows us to "wake up," to push aside the things that somehow fill our to-do lists (but in all reality, are not meaningful) and direct our energy and actions toward the important things in our life, the ones that fill our lives with meaning, purpose, and happiness.

Case Study: Randy Pausch

Randy Pausch was a teacher in every sense of the word. Beginning in 1988, he served as a college professor, eventually training future computer scientists at the prestigious Carnegie Mellon University. He was passionate about his work and imparting knowledge to his students. But in 2006, Pausch was diagnosed with pancreatic cancer. He tried to fight it, but within a year, he was told his disease was terminal.

Unwilling to be denied of his life–even in his closing days–Pausch agreed to teach his ultimate lesson. Carnegie Mellon invited the professor to join a very special speaking series. The program, which had long been called "The Last Lecture," was devised to force invited presenters to think about what they would say if they were on their deathbed and were given one last occasion to offer wise words.

But unlike other speakers who gave their speeches hypothetically, Pausch was actually taking a final opportunity to explain what he'd learned on this planet. He titled his last lecture "Really Achieving Your Childhood Dreams," and for more than an hour, he captivated a packed audience with the goals he'd set for himself as a child, and how he diligently worked to fulfill them throughout his life.

Despite his terminal diagnosis, Pausch was articulate,

funny, and unflinching about making the most of one's precious time and appropriately channeling a person's energies toward a central objective. He also took the opportunity to thank his wife and children, parents and friends, co-workers and mentors. (He even had a cake brought out to wish his wife a happy birthday.)

When asked, "What kind of person should I try to be?" Pausch answered: "The kind of person other people seem to want to help. That strikes me as a pretty good answer."

A key takeaway Pausch talked about was re-programming your intentions if they don't serve your ambitions and life purpose. "We cannot change the cards we are dealt; just how we play the hand," he explained.

Along with emotionally touching all those who attended the session, Pausch's lecture was filmed and, almost immediately, became a viral sensation. Pausch proved so good at teaching, that, even after his supposed last lecture, he wasn't done providing sage insight. Before his death, he would go on to write a best-selling book based on the event called *The Last Lecture*(2).

All told, his efforts inspired countless individuals to redesign their personal blueprints and develop their own purpose that could make a difference for their family, society, and themselves. As one pundit wrote about Pausch: "Countless people were inspired to start chasing after their dreams and change their lives. His positivity and can-do mentality was infectious."

Pausch was a rare individual: He intuitively knew what he wanted from a young age and went after it. On July 25, 2008, he succumbed to the cancer at age forty-seven. But thanks to his approach to pursue what was important to him, when Pausch reached the end, he had no regrets about the choices he made.

Now it's your turn:

Write five things that you would never want to regret about on your deathbed:

1. _____

   _____

2. _____

   _____

3. _____

   _____

4. _____

   _____

5. _____

   _____

CHAPTER 4

The Fear of Death

"As a day well spent brings happy sleep, so a life well spent brings happy death."

—Leonardo da Vinci

Death is the great equalizer. We all die. Despite this, most of us still harbor a great deal of anxiety around the idea of death. To some, it is manifested as a feeling of dread or apprehension; others will try to push it from their minds completely.

Death terrifies many people to the point of chronic anxiety that is the core of several mental health disorders, including panic disorder and depressive disorders.

This is due in large part to the fact that we're too scared to talk about it. A ComRes survey from 2014[3] found that 80% of people in Britain are uncomfortable talking about death, and just 33% had written a will, a clear indicator that people simply don't want to be reminded that they'll die.

> We fear death and are afraid to contemplate it, so we are missing important lessons it can provide.

Ernest Becker, in his Pulitzer prize winning book *The Denial of Death*,[4] explains that to free oneself of death anxiety, nearly everyone chooses the path of repression. We bury the idea of death deep in the subconscious and then busy ourselves with daily activities and entertainment to fill our living time. Eventually, when it becomes apparent that our days are numbered, those repressed anxieties begin welling up into our consciousness and we proceed to live our final years under a dark and increasingly foreboding shadow. No one's final time on Earth should be spent processing repressed fears.

A social psychological theory, called Terror Management Theory (TMT), is one way to understand how this anxiety influences our behavior and sense of self. According to this theory, we manage our fear of death by creating a sense of permanence and meaning in life. We focus on personal achievements and accomplishments of loved ones; we take endless photos to create enduring memories; we may attend church and believe in an afterlife. These behaviors bolster our self-esteem and can help us feel empowered against death.

The fear of death is so innate in us that even children express fear of death. Take for example Nate, a five-year-old living in San Diego, California. Nate's mother described an incident she experienced with him one evening: "I was giving him a bath one night. He swam up and down in the bath and then told me: 'I don't want to be dead, ever; I don't want to die.' After I soothed and reassured him that he wouldn't die for a long time, Nate smiled back and said, 'I've been worried, can I play again?.'"

We all are worried about death in one way or another, but the good news is that we are probably worried too much. A group of researchers[5] decided to analyze the writing of regular bloggers with either terminal cancer or amyotrophic lateral sclerosis (ALS) disease who later died over the course of the study and compared it to blog posts written by a group of participants who were told to imagine they had been diagnosed with terminal cancer and had only a few months to live. They looked for general feelings of positivity and negativity, and words describing positive and negative emotions including happiness, fear, and terror. The results were that blog posts from the terminally ill were found to have considerably more positive words and fewer negative ones than those imagining they were dying–and their use of positive language increased as they got closer to death. One of the researchers, Kurt Gray, explained the results: "The dying know things are getting more serious, and there's some kind of acceptance and focus on the positive as they know they don't have much time left."

As you can see, we might fear death too much but apparently, we get better at accepting death as we age. A meta-analysis study[6] found that fear of death grows in the first half of life, but between the ages of sixty-one to eighty-seven, it recedes to a stable, manageable level.

But how does awareness of death effect our behavior and

quality of life? According to research[7] done on socioemotional selectivity theory, older people are more present-oriented than younger people, and are more selective in who they spend time with, sticking mostly with family and longer-term, close friends. These studies have shown that elderly also are more forgiving, more caring toward others, while being less concerned about enhancing themselves.

So what can we do to reduce our fear of death?

A 2016[8] study identified that following the fear of death, public speaking is the 2nd item on the list of people's greatest fears. How is it, then, that so many people are still able to engage in this activity, if so many of us claim to fear it so greatly?

Practice!

And this idea of practice extends not just to public speaking, but to pretty much any endeavor we undertake. A professional athlete, a superstar musician, a best-selling author—they all have to practice, to get better, to get used to what they are doing. To become comfortable with it.

> Practice eliminates the fear of unknown. The same is true with death – simulate it and your anxiety will dramatically reduce.

Your experience with death should be the same.

The more you practice it, the more you'll feel comfortable with it. Each time you practice, you'll experience death from a different angle and see it from a different possible situation. You'll notice a mindset shift as you start feeling more comfortable with your eventual passing away.

Anxiety about death can also stem from worrying about those we'll leave behind. How will our children cope without a parent? Will our partner be able to recover emotionally from our passing? Will the family have enough money to continue to live the kind of life they deserve?

These are all valid worries which add stress to the thought of death. It's often just easier to not think about it at all, rather than face the hard questions.

The good news is that, while we can't control when or how we leave this world, we can certainly control the state of what we leave behind. Many people feel a sense of relief when they get their after-death affairs in order—even if they have many decades of healthy life ahead of them. They know should the unwanted happen unexpectedly, their affairs will be in order, nothing will be left for chance, and their family's future will be secure.

When my first child, Tal, was born in 2007, the first thing my wife and I did was create a living will, which sorts all legal, custodial, and financial issues regarding our children in case we die. It's just one less thing either of us has to worry about, as, there are clear instructions on how to handle our assets and who takes cares of our children.

Part of practicing death is about death *awareness*—shifting from anxiety or anguish to acceptance. Practicing death encompasses dealing with fear and some anxiety. But just beyond this very natural feeling lies a more meaningful, profound, and life-changing realization—a relief at having faced it and a greater commitment to affirmative action; a re-doubling of the effort to live fully, to clarify your priorities, and bring your deeds in line with your values. Practicing death leads to serenity, reduction of stress, reduced anxiety, and an overall happier life.

Case Study: Alex C.

There were two things I noticed when I first saw Alex: his bright young face covered with long, dripping brown hair and his uneven walk as he dragged his right foot forward. Alex was twenty-six when he participated in my workshop and we stayed in touch since. I was very moved by his story, which he agreed to share with the readers of this book:

> *I was born in France and was always a very active child. I used to play soccer and dreamt of joining the France team to win the World Cup. When I turned sixteen, I started surfing, which quickly became the love of my life. I used to spend every summer on the beach and whenever the surf was up, I'd be out there, even if I risked being late to work.*
>
> *Two years ago, I began to notice that something was wrong with my right leg. When I was in the water, it wasn't kicking as fast as my left leg and sometimes, it just hung there. I went to my doctor*

to check it out and he sent me to the hospital for a series of tests. Two weeks later, I was diagnosed with a neuromuscular disorder called muscular dystrophy, which causes muscle loss over time. I was told that there is no cure for it and that it will grow worse as time goes by and that at some point I'll lose the ability to walk and be bound to a wheelchair for the rest of my life.

I was shocked and in disbelief. Since then, I developed a love-hate relationship with my body: I see myself as a young, attractive surfer who loves life and wants to do great things, yet, I hate that my body is falling apart every day. In the last six months, the deterioration of my condition has increased dramatically and things I could do a month ago I can't do anymore. I can no longer stand to urinate, which is very embarrassing, as I can't even use the urinals in many public places. My body is falling apart and I can't stop it.

My self-esteem also suffered. I don't feel comfortable dating, and spending time with my friends has changed, as many of the things we used to do together are no longer possible.

I know that my body can't be healed and will only get worse over time, but I'm struggling every day to accept this new reality and stop the self-pity.

I found myself asking a couple of times a day: Why me? What did I do to deserve this?

I heard about the Death Practice workshop from a friend who participated and recommended it. I didn't have many expectations and was more concerned about my physical limitations. Luckily, I just needed to lay down and do the set of breathing exercises. It helped me experience something very unique that really changed my life.

I saw myself lying on my death bed, my body much older. I was surrounded by several of my friends and a beautiful, mature woman with golden hair, who was hugging two boys that I later realized were my sons. I saw a wheelchair folded in the corner of the room and I felt a huge relief that I have a family of my own. I wasn't afraid of my upcoming death; I was actually elated that I had a normal family and two kids and a beautiful wife. My boys were tall, looked healthy and I was so proud. I was euphoric that my life wasn't lived in vain. I became very emotional and was tearing up from happiness. I didn't care my children saw me crying— I was just so happy to be there, seeing them.

Then my body started to be carried toward a bright light above me that extended way beyond a normal ceiling. It kept pulling me up, even as I reached my hand toward my family. I knew after a few seconds it was my time to leave them behind to live their lives. I felt content and in peace to part from life and this is when I woke up.

It was such a transformational experience—my life turned 180 degrees. From self-pity about my degenerating situation, I've now begun accepting that I'll live in a wheelchair. Instead of fighting it and delaying it, I actually began visualizing myself in it and was looking forward to that day in which I'll start my new life, the life in which I find my wife and raise a family.

> **Simulating my death was truly transformational, it changed my life from self-pity to full acceptance.**

It has been ten months since the workshop and I'm now in a wheelchair, as my right leg is 100% paralyzed and my left leg is only 40% functional. But I'm happy with my life. I've started dating again and have a positive approach—as much one can have—about the disease and my prospects in life.

Practicing death helps me put my disease in perspective. It is horrible to find yourself incapacitated at such a young age, but placed in perspective of life as a whole, I am still the same handsome, smart, and life-loving person I was—more importantly, I'm alive. So while I'm still here, I'm going to make the best out of it, make my future wife happy, and raise a family.

I owe this insight to the death practice which I keep

doing twice or so a month. It keeps me grounded on what I have in life and I'm grateful for that.

Now it's your turn:

Write three fears you have about your death:

1. _____

   _____

2. _____

   _____

3. _____

   _____

CHAPTER 5

Benefits of Practicing Death

"Analysis of death is not for the sake of becoming fearful but to appreciate this precious lifetime."
—The Dalai Lama

The English writer Samuel Johnson once said, "When you know you're to be hanged in a fortnight, it concentrates the mind wonderfully." The theologian Thomas Merton added that in considering any important decision in life, and certainly in considering your priorities in life, it's imperative to "consult your death."

At first glance, practicing death sounds morbid, dark, and otherwise unsavory. When I advocate for contemplating death, it's not for the purpose of wanting to die. Rather, on the contrary, what we are actually doing is focusing on *life*. This practice is a way to utilize a powerful and eye-opening experience to gain hidden and invaluable insight, which, if acted upon, can improve your life.

Stephen Covey's second habit[9] of highly effective people is: "Begin with the end in mind," by which he means that we all should have a clear sense of where we're headed to be effective with our lives. It is especially true in regard to the extent of your life. You need to understand the end, to be able to fully live the now.

> When you keep the end in mind, you can direct your life and become the person you really want to be.

In the next chapter, we'll discuss in detail the technique you can use to practice death. But before we get into that, here are the main benefits you'll gain by utilizing this technique:

1) Death is the ultimate clarifier – it will distill your priorities

When you'll analyze the sights that you'll experience during your death-practice, you will recognize and be able to eliminate those activities, both large and small, that don't pass the "hanged in a fortnight" test. By asking yourself, "Does this activity takes me toward or away from the things that really matter to me?" you'll gain a better understanding of where to direct your energy so you can remain focused on the things that truly matter.

If what matters to you is spending time with your young children, but the promotion you were just offered means you won't get home until long after the kids are asleep, then maybe the right thing is to negotiate a work schedule that enables you to be with your family in the evenings, or, simply pass on it. Remember, you don't want to find yourself later in life regretting that you missed the childhood of your children.

70% of adults hate their job.[10] If you are one of them, ask yourself the following question: *Would I stay in my current job if I only had one year to live?* If the answer is "No way!" then why are you working there in the first place? Remember—It's never too late to get your priorities straight. For many, simply quitting their job isn't an option due to financial obligations or debt burden. That said, you should use the insights from your death practice to begin a personal introspection process to identify your passion and interests. Hopefully, it will allow you, over time, to seek another job, or start your own enterprise, one which brings you joy (or at least one you don't hate!)

2) Death provides a sense of urgency to do the things you really want to do

Imagine knowing the day you would die. Like a milk carton with an expiration date, if we were privy to the exact moment our lives would end, we would undoubtedly ensure we'll try to accomplish everything we wanted to do before that date arrived.

This is why deadlines work—you have a specific time that you need to have something completed by. Likewise, in life, we will all face our deadline, though we don't know precisely when that will be. By ignoring our "deadline" and living as if it's always far, far away we postpone doing the things that make us feel that we are truly "living" our lives. By practicing death, we have the opportunity to realize, and more importantly, take immediate action, to achieve the important things we really want to achieve in life. The ancient Egyptians used to bring a human skull to every important political gathering and ceremonies—to help attendees remember their fortune to be alive and clarify their decision in light of their eventual ending.

> We live as if we have all the time in the world – letting years go by unnoticed. If you were told that this month is your last, suddenly things will get done!

As times goes by, postponement of passions and callings is a less and less a viable option, so starting to practice death earlier in life has tremendous benefits.

When you're on the clock, you accomplish more. If you don't really know what you want to do in life, just Google the phrase "Things I want to do before I die" and peruse the lists people have compiled—it will give you enough ideas for a lifetime.

3) Practicing death reduces your fear of death

We are afraid to die, but perhaps that is because, as a society, we do not talk about death. As seen earlier, the fear of

Death is ranked high on human's list of fears. People who are required to speak regularly in front of an audience, are not born without a stage fright. They confront their innate stage fright by practicing public speaking until they master their delivery. They start small, presenting in front of their partner or a friend then move to small groups of strangers. Overtime, they increase their confidence and are able to speak in front of thousands of people. In so many aspects of life "practice makes perfect" so why not apply it to practicing death to make that feared moment less daunting.

Many of your family members and friends will remember you as you were in your parting moments. Do you want it to be a memory of a strong, confident person who is at ease and in control of his destiny or do you want to be remembered with a frightened look on your face?

Practicing death will allow you to arrive in the moment of truth in control, having practiced for this hundreds of times. Your lack of fear will be evident to your closest friends and family, and that is the memory you want to leave behind.

4) It will enhance your happiness, expand your acceptance, and deepen your gratitude for life

Many of us understand death intellectually but not emotionally. The most consistent benefit of practicing death is acceptance—accepting yourself, the life you live, and that you will, one day, die.

Studies have demonstrated that awareness of death increases expressions of compassion, tolerance, and empathy. A Florida State University[11] study showed that just being physically near a cemetery affects how willing people are to help a stranger. Those who walked through a cemetery were 40% more likely to help someone than those who walked only a block away.

More generally, what mortality can teach us is a deeper gratitude for life and a keener appreciation for the beauties and pleasures of the world, which will allow us to focus more on the relationships that matter most to us. When you're feeling deeply alive, there just doesn't seem to be the same block between you and others.

> When you really understand what you can lose, you finally start appreciating what you already have.

Try this the next time you visit the ocean. Look at the huge rock slabs and the vast ocean. Think about the immensity of time that took the ocean to carve the cliffs around you. If you live far from the ocean, lift your head during a clear night and watch the stars uninterrupted, for ten minutes. Do you grasp the big picture?

When we look at things using a long-term lens, it puts our short life in perspective. To put it bluntly: We are insignificant, in the grand scheme of things. Accepting this insignificance allows us to become more humble, compassionate, and alive.

5) It enables you to understand and support dying loved ones

During our lifetime, we all are going to experience the death of loved ones, be it older parents, sick friends and family members. If you care about them and want to understand what they are experiencing, there is nothing better than really putting yourself in their condition and practicing death.

Your insights and calm demeanor will be highly valued and can help them immensely through their death process by reducing their fear and suffering.

Practicing death can be a great source of meaning, the enzyme of your drives and passions, as death is the brute existential fact that injects urgency.

It is a catalyst to making life-altering changes. Once practiced regularly, it can help you live a healthier and more positive life.

Make a commitment to practice death once a week for ten minutes, explore your passions and write a "bucket list" with all of the amazing things that you want to do before you die.

Remember: If you are busy living, you won't be worried about dying.

Case Study: Katerina W.

I joined to the Death Practice workshop by coincidence. One day I was shopping at a mini-market and started conversing with another girl as we waited in line. She told me about a workshop taking place that afternoon. I was at such a low point in my life I decided to give it a try. I feel so grateful that I met her that afternoon, as it literally brought a lost father to my son's life!

Just a year earlier, while traveling in Asia, I met Christian, a forty-year-old Swis guy that I fell in love with. I was thirty-seven, working in marketing at a high-tech company in London, and he was a free-soul, traveling around the world. We spent an amazing two months traveling together and really connecting on a personal level when he had to head back to Switzerland for family matters.

Two days after we parted ways I found out I was pregnant. How the hell did I get into this mess?

As a child, I had never met my father. I was born out of wedlock and my mother never tried to reach out to the person who impregnated her. It was the 70s, so I grew up in a household in which men used to come and go and I would see new faces during breakfast all the time. I got used to it and grew up just fine without any fatherly figure.

For me, men meant one thing: trouble. I never trusted them and they were never associated with a sense of security; quite the contrary—they represented chaos.

Therefore, when I learned I was pregnant, I immediately knew I'd be dealing with this alone. The thought of getting Christian involved in raising the child never crossed my mind; why did I need additional trouble? And besides, he'll run away from it, so why bother getting him involved?

He called me a week later to see what I was up to. We spoke for half an hour before I had the courage to mention, apologetically, that I was pregnant. I thought he had the right to know.

It caught him by surprise. None of us expected this to happen. But although he was shaken up initially, he didn't behave the way I expected him to. He didn't tell me to get an abortion so we could avoid this unintended annoyance and continue with our previous lives. Instead, he was genuinely happy about the news and, on the spot, offered to fly back the next day to help. Who does that?

I was taken aback by this rush of excitement, as I was underwhelmed by the whole situation myself. Now I had another person to deal with.

Christian's behavior was really different than the behavior of other men I knew. Although I told him not to come, he left everything behind, flew to England, and rented an apartment across the street from mine. Not for stalking me, but to help me. He made grocery runs, insisted to come to every ultrasound check (although I told him he didn't need to bother) and purchased top of the line baby clothes and accessories for the newborn. He was all-in.

Nevertheless, during the week before we first spoke, I already planned the whole thing in my mind. I was going to be a super-mom and raise this child by myself as I couldn't count on Christian or any other man to be there long-term for me. So I persistently pushed Christian away.

In the beginning, there were subtle and gentle cues, but as we got closer to the delivery I made it very clear to him that I didn't think I loved him and didn't want him to be around me or my child.

Still, he tenderly held my hand when I screamed in pain while delivering my son, Jonah.

After the delivery, I kept pushing Christian away as the responsibility of caring for Jonah became real. Eventually I told him that I never loved him and it was all a big mistake. I told him that I don't want to see him anymore!

Finally, I drove Christian away and, in the process, I broke his heart.

Christian flew back home, and it took me several months to realize what I have done. But by then, it was too late to bring Christian back to our lives. I shattered his heart to a thousand pieces and he was trying to heal. I became that evil character from a tragic love story.

This is when I ran into that girl at the mini-market. It was probably the lowest point in my life. I was stressed out and depressed, a clueless first-time single mom carrying around a ten-month-old baby, looking for anything that could guide my way out of this bottomless pit called life. Not surprising that practicing death sounded like a great afternoon activity; maybe I could master my death there and be done with it all. I signed up for the workshop.

But during the workshop, when I practiced my death, I had an amazing spiritual experience. I saw myself lying on a bed in a bamboo cabin somewhere deep in the jungle. Jonah and Christian were there, looking at me with comforting faces. We spoke softly, Jonah throwing jokes around; he had become such a handsome young man.

Christian looked older with salt-and-pepper hair and a pair of glasses I'd never seen him wearing before. When I looked closely at him, I saw he was crying. Why? Only then did I realize why—they were holding my hand. I was on my death bed, at home, about to leave them.

But I wasn't afraid; I was actually happy. Happy to see my baby grown up so much, happy to feel secure in the presence of Christian, happy to realize that we made it back to become a family.

Then, I remember closing my eyes to rest. I felt my body floating in the air for few seconds before starting to crumble into whiffs of dust, my spirit moving quickly to somewhere else. I felt elated, secure, and peaceful. I wanted to hold that feeling forever when I started hearing chimes of a bell which brought me back into consciousness. I wasn't dying, I was just practicing death, and it felt so good.

That evening, I knew exactly what I need to do to relive that feeling. If I ever want to have that peaceful and secure sentiment in life, I needed Christian back in my arms so I could hug him tight. He didn't want to run in the first place, so why did I push him away?

Over the next few weeks I reached out to Christian and we had multiple heart-to-heart conversations. He was afraid to get hurt again which, I totally

> Simulating death enables us to look at our life in context. It provides new perspective and, usually, profound realizations.

understood. I still begged him to give me a second chance.

We agreed to give it a try. He flew over, rented his own place, and we slowly built a schedule that gradually improved the trust between us.

It's been six months since we got back together and I'm very optimistic. The wound in his heart hasn't fully healed and we are still working on our relationship, but we are doing it together, the three of us.

I believe now that he's here for the long run. I'm thankful to the death practice that helped me realize what was truly valuable and pushed me to overcome my fear and go and get it. I see Christian's presence at my death bed every time I practice death and my heart is filled with joy—and for that I am really grateful.

Now it's your turn:

Write two things that you can benefit from by practicing death—focus on how you can grow as a person:

1. _____

   _____

2. _____

   _____

CHAPTER 6

Technique for Practicing Death

"Practice Dying."
—Plato's final instructions to his disciples before his own death

While Plato's recommendation to his disciples was more philosophical in nature, it demonstrates the importance of the practice. This chapter will provide a simple technique which everyone can do, in the comfort of your home, and will take only ten minutes a week.

How this practice was developed? Like many good things in life—by chance.

I practice yoga for many years, all over the world: New York, California, Israel, and recently in Ubud, Bali, which is considered a mecca for yogis and spiritual seekers. I don't consider myself a yoga fanatic or even an especially good practitioner: I'm a normal guy who was told about the benefits of exercise and felt that as my body becomes older and less able to do the extreme sports I once used to do (marathons, Ironman, snowboarding, to name a few) doing yoga twice a week won't kill me and, might even, keep my evolving beer-belly in check.

If you're unfamiliar with yoga, it's a practice that includes movement of the body in certain poses that improves flexibility, muscle alignment and core strength. It also serves as a sort of meditation, as the movements are done at a relatively slow pace, encouraging practitioners to focus on their breath and mind.

But the practice can also be excruciating and physically exhausting (especially if you join a Power Yoga class) and usually twenty minutes into it, I find myself dripping sweat and using a small towel to dry my face. As yoga practices usually last forty-five to ninety minutes, you can imagine how you might feel at the end of such practice – I feel pretty exhausted.

It is common to end each yoga class with a cool down, in a pose called *shavasana*. The term comes from the Sanskrit language and means "corpse pose" (shava, meaning "corpse," and asana, meaning "pose").

For this pose, you lie on your back, legs comfortably spread and arms relaxed alongside the body, palms facing up. You close your eyes and fully relax.

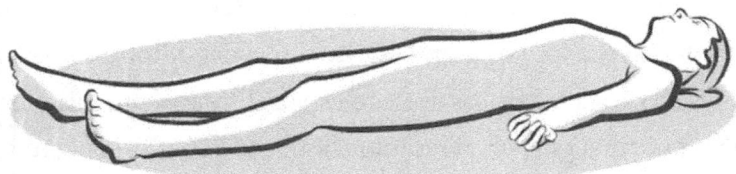

Usually the yoga instructor will put on calming background music and after three to four minutes, with the students all fully relaxed or semi-asleep, the instructor will ring a tiny bell to signal the students to re-enter awareness and move to a sitting position before the class ends.

Because this pose is done at the end of the yoga practice, when my body is exhausted, I used to use these few precious moments of relaxation to close my eyes and think about my work to-do-list and prepare myself for the rest of the day.

Until... something very different and powerful happened.

It was the end of Saturday morning class and we were instructed to transition into the shavasana pose, which I gladly followed. I prepped my body on the yoga mat with my face up to the ceiling, spread my arms and legs to a comfortable position, closed my eyes, and...

Instead of creating a to-do list in my head, I suddenly saw myself looking up at the faces of my children and my beautiful wife. They were all looking at me from above, leaning on a side bar of a hospital bed. Everything was serene, peaceful, and quiet, enveloped in a bright white aura. My daughter and my wife were crying, which concerned me. *Why are they crying?* But then it dawned on me—I'm dying!

Interestingly enough, the thought of dying didn't fill me with fear. Instead, a very serene and calming feeling filled every inch of my body—*I'm going to die, and I'm totally fine with it.*

In a way, a huge burden was lifted—no more financial

pressures, no more stressing over emails and dealing with an annoying boss. All of my irritations became irrelevant and now I could focus on saying goodbye to the people I love.

> When your mind and body are well-conditioned, internal wisdom can surface up revealing invaluable insights.

I looked at the weeping eyes of my daughter and reached to gently wipe away her tears. I calmed her and asked her not to cry, told her how much I love her, and that I will always love her and be with her forever. I was an absent father to her, tied to my job for many years of her life, and now I regretted not spending more quality time playing with her.

I asked my eleven-year-old son, who held back his emotions, to take my role as the man of the family. To help his mom as much as he can by doing as she asks, even if he doesn't always want to. He nodded with understanding.

I tried to reassure my children that everything is going to be fine when I'm gone and that Mom will take care of them. I promised them that life will be pretty much the same, just with me not being around to annoy them—and I got a gentle chuckle and smile, which made me happy inside.

In the background, I saw the faces of my parents, siblings, and few of my friends, some of whom I hadn't spoken with in years. Yet I felt nothing but calm and acceptance that my role in this world had run its course and I could peacefully pass away. It was an exhilarating feeling that I wanted to hold onto forever.

Suddenly, the sound of a ringing bell drifted into my consciousness, followed a few seconds later, by a stronger chime. I immediately remembered where I was—not in a hospital bed surrounded by my loved ones but on a yoga mat surrounded by other sweating and couple snoring yogis!

I did feel some sadness at the abrupt end of this magical moment of serenity and connection with my loved ones, but I now found myself full of a new and invigorating energy. The yoga session ended, I rolled up the mat, and walked out of the studio, analyzing the experience.

That I had not spent more time with my daughter bothered me the most, and prompted me to prioritize my time and initiate activities with her that would allow us more quality time together.

I also remembered the face of one of the friends I saw around my deathbed. It surprised me to see him there; his name was Tomer, a good old friend from high school who we spend most of my late childhood and early adulthood together but then each of us moved to live in different countries and eventually we lost touch.

With the image of his face affixed in my mind, I decided to drop everything, picked up my phone and called him. While it was really late in Canada, where he lived, we spoke for more than an hour, catching each other up on everything that had been happening in the time we had not spoken. We both had much to share, including the news that he's expecting a third child. We were both surprised that I didn't know considering how close we were in the past where we shared everything with each other. It seemed hard to believe that so much time had passed since we had last seen each other. But that is life—so easy to get caught up in the day-to-day hustle and bustle that we can easily lose touch with the people we once considered our closest friends.

I also found renewed energy for projects I had been putting off. I'd been planning to launch an app that connects donors and people in need. For months I'd been procrastinating, always finding a new reason to postpone starting to write the business plan, but now, I had a real urge to make it happen. I headed to a coffee shop, pulled out my laptop, and started working on it.

> The daily grind prevents us from pursuing our passion and purpose. Practicing death injects new energy that allows us to live to our true potential.

It was only 11AM and already an extremely productive day; the few minutes of death-like experience launched a new stream of energy that made me reach out to a forgotten friend, prioritize my calendar to spend time with my daughter, and get started on something that I had kept putting off. I felt alive in a way I hadn't felt in a long time.

If this experience could be so transformational, amplifying

my energy and making me happy about changes I'm taking to improve my life why shouldn't I keep doing it?

To be honest, in the past I used to view yoga classes as a chore, so I went infrequently, but since that experience, I look forward to my yoga classes. Not because of the yoga itself but because of few minutes at the end, during shavasana, when I get to practice death.

So the great news is that you don't need to go to yoga classes to engage in this practice (sigh of relief...)

Practicing death is actually quite easy and can be done in the comfort of your home.

The practice is 100% safe and was vetted by many psychologists that I've interviewed as part of the research for this book. The practice method and its potential benefits are aligned with years of psychological research regarding confronting fears and handling phobias.

So here we go . . .

To imitate the shavasana pose, lay on your bed, a mat, or a blanket. Make sure the area in which you are practicing is quiet—close the door, silence your phone, and do anything else necessary to minimize possible distractions. If possible, set an alarm with a gentle chime sound to ring in ten minutes. It will gently awaken you from the death practice in a peaceful and serene way. Some practitioners swear by the alarm; otherwise they might fall asleep, particularly if they practice death early in the morning or late in the evening.

Once in your quiet space, find a comfortable position while laying on your back. Use a pillow if you'd like and place it under your head or under your legs for support. Spread your legs slightly and let your feet lay relaxed on the bed. Extend your hands to the side of your body, palms facing either up or down— whatever makes you feel more relaxed and doesn't require energy to maintain. The idea is to relax your muscles and enable your mind to focus on the experience.

Close your eyes. For an easier transition, you can place an eye cover or small towel over your eyes to prevent changes in the ambient light that could disturb you.

Once you're comfortable, begin the following breathing sequence. The goal of the breathing sequence is to oxidize your body and bring it to a similar condition that a sixty-minute yoga class would have brought (without the sweat).

- ▶ Take twenty-five very deep breaths in, and exhale rapidly, letting 80% of the air out quickly.
- ▶ Once you exhaled the last breath, hold your breath for one minute or until you can't hold it anymore (the average person can hold their breath for two minutes, so a minute should be easy).
- ▶ Do this sequence three more times for a total of

seventy-five breaths (twenty-five deep breaths and exhales followed by one minute of holding your breath).

You might feel tingling in your fingers and toes and a slight pounding in your head. These are all very natural and welcomed effects of the exercise, so don't be concerned. It means that your body has a good amount of oxygen and that you are ready to begin the main part of the practice.

Once your body is full of oxygen, it is primed to let your mind focus on your death experience.

> ▸ Mindfully, initiate the practice by seeding your death, basically imagining in your mind your last moments wherever that is. It can be in your bed at home, at a hospital, or anywhere you feel that you most likely will be at the moment of truth.
> ▸ Let your mind slip into the last moments of your life . . .
>   - Look up and see who is there beside you. Family members? Friends? Someone you have not seen in a long time?
>   - Don't focus on who is not there or who you might have wanted to be there for your picture-perfect parting moment, but instead, absorb the picture that comes to your mind, organically. If your mind wanders off to ordinary thoughts, just bring it back

Condition your mind to enter a state of letting go and seed the thought of your parting moments.

to the last scene you remember from your death experience. Getting sidetracked is normal—the mind works in strange ways—so instead of getting angry or frustrated, just gently steer your focus back to the practice.

- Is the mood calm and serene? Or tense? Sad? Something else entirely?
- What the people around you seem to feel? Are they in despair, or celebrating the last few minutes of your life with you?
- What sorts of things are they saying to you?
- What do you want to tell them? Do you have parting words to share with everyone as a group or do you want to address each person individually?
- How do you feel?
- Do you have any feeling of regret? Make sure to remember it.

Let yourself be fully immersed in the experience until you hear the sound of the alarm you set before you started the practice (or if you haven't set an alarm, until you feel the experience came its natural end).

▶ Transition to awakening: when you hear the chimes, while keeping your eyes closed, start to gently move your fingers and toes to get blood flowing back into your limbs.
▶ Stretch:

- Move your arms above your head, stretching gently for few seconds.
- Now fold your legs toward your belly, holding them in both arms and squeezing for few seconds.
- With the legs hugged to your chest, rock back and forth and from left to right several times to get your body back in motion.
▶ Transition to Sitting: Once you are ready, roll to your right side and slowly come to a seated position, eyes still closed.
▶ Clam down: Take three deep breaths and then exhale slowly.
▶ Transition to Life: Open your eyes slowly and get accustomed to the light of the room. If you feel very emotional, remain sited for as long as you need until you feel ready to continue your day.

You have just completed your first death practice, something most will find to be a very profound experience.

You might be flooded with emotions—this is normal, and very common. It is important that you take a couple of minutes to calm your mind before rushing out for your daily routine. Allowing yourself a few minutes to reflect also helps to internalize and analyze what just happened. It will crystalize what can be learned from the experience and clarify the things you can change in your life–the pinnacle of personal growth.

It is recommended to keep a pen and a small notebook next to where you do your practice. If during the practice (or the post-experience analysis) you have a revelation regarding time priorities, a relationship, or just a thought you want to capture, having a notebook handy means you can jot these points down before you continue on with your day.

Practicing death takes no more than ten minutes for most people. But I encourage you to experiment, as some people benefit from a longer breathing prelude and some people prefer a shorter one. A few practitioners have informed me that they tend to fall asleep if their death experience lasts too long or if they are tired from a long day at work. So, test when the best time is for you to do the practice—is it early morning or later in the day? Try a longer and a shorter breathing session and see what works best for you.

When you practice death, you apply what psychologists call *systematic desensitization*, a behavioral technique often used with fears and phobias. It involves gradually exposing yourself to the thing you fear most and simultaneously relaxing. In other words, go slowly, take deep breaths, and do this practice regularly, at least once a week. Most of us do have very busy lives, but ten minutes, once a week, is certainly manageable for almost everyone.

You can try varying scenarios to test your Death Practice and achieve new insights from

> By practicing death once a week, for just 10 minutes, you'll achieve all the amazing benefits.

Technique for Practicing Death • 53

the practice. Try different mindset "seeds" when you go into your future practice. Below are some scenarios for seeding that you can try:
- Your final moments in 5 years from now
- Imagine the ideal death situation for you, where you'll be, who you will be with?
- You feel a heart attack in your favorite restaurant while dining with your family and medical emergency is delayed, what do you tell them?
- Your final moments in 20 years from now
- What is the worst situation you can image you'll die? If you prepare yourself for it, everything else will feel so much better.

Now it's your turn:

Take ten minutes tomorrow morning and commit to doing your first death practice.

Write below what you have experienced. How did you feel at the end of the practice?

_____

_____

_____

_____

CHAPTER 7

Spirituality in Practicing Death

"We all owe God a death"

—Shakespeare

Practicing death can have a profound spiritual element to it, especially if you believe in re-incarnation. Some of us do. Others believe death is the Final Outcome, and once your life is over, that's it. Still others are unsure of what they believe. If you take this practice as a spiritual journey, be prepared for a wild ride, as practicing death can evoke a vast mystery of memories and strong, sometimes unexpected, feelings.

> **Practicing death can be an invaluable spiritual journey to believers.**

But know that practicing death does not mean that you should act like a monk and lock yourself up in a monastery while pursuing enlightenment. Not at all. The spiritual elements of the practice can be achieved anywhere. This spiritual process will clarify your own priorities regarding the time you want to spend with specific fellow humans in the time you have left in life.

This chapter provides a very high-level and superficial overview on how different religions and beliefs view death. It is intentionally broad-based and presents a wide range of approaches to death. You are invited to read, expose yourself to other approaches for personal growth, or just skip to the section representing your belief.

▶ Buddhism

According to Tenzin Palmo,[12] a Buddhist teacher who spent twelve years living in a remote cave in the Himalayas (three of them in pure meditation), death is a stage of transition. It is "merely an exchange of a rugged and old body of this life with a new and young body of the next, like changing your clothes when they are old and worn out. Buddhists see death as a process and not as an end."

The Buddha himself recommended death (corpse) meditation. His students were taught to say about their own bodies, "This body, too, such is its nature, such is its future, such its unavoidable fate."

The Tibetan Book of the Dead[13] (Bar Do Thos Grol), composed in the 8th century, describes a conception of postmortem existence. Over twelve days, the deceased person is given explanations of what he or she sees and experiences after death and is guided through innumerable visions of the realms beyond to reach eventual liberation, or, failing that, a safe rebirth.

Paradoxically, death meditation is actually intended

as a key to better living. Contemporary Buddhist practitioners spend hours on their meditation cushions experiencing death in their healthy bodies. It makes disciples aware of the transitory nature of their own physical lives and stimulates a re-alignment between momentary desires and existential goals. In other words, it makes one ask, "Am I making the right use of my scarce and precious life?"

> Death meditation is not new and is practiced for 1300 years.

Geshe Kelsang, a Buddhist monk, meditation teacher, and scholar says, "Contemplating our own death will inspire us to use our life wisely by developing the inner refuge of spiritual realizations; otherwise we shall have no ability to protect ourselves from the suffering of death and what lies beyond. Moreover, when someone close to us is dying, such as a parent or friend, we shall be powerless to help them because we shall not know how; and we shall experience sadness and frustration at our inability to be of genuine help. Preparing for death is one of the kindest and wisest things we can do both for ourselves and others."

▶ Hinduism

Most Hindus believe that humans are in a cycle of death and rebirth called *samsara*. When a person dies, their *atman* (the eternal self) is reborn in a different body.

Some believe rebirth happens directly at death; others believe that an atman may exist in other realms. An atman may enter *swarg* (heaven) or *narak* (hell) for a period before rebirth. Hindus also believe in karma or *intentional action*, where good or bad actions in life lead to positive or negative merit, thereby determining the atman's rebirth.

Some Hindus believe that humans may be reborn in animal form, and that rebirth from human to animal form only occurs if an atman has repeatedly failed to learn lessons as a human.

Living life according to teachings in the scriptures will eventually lead to *moksha* (enlightenment or liberation). Some Hindu scriptures describe moksha as the atman becoming absorbed with Brahman (the god from where each atman is believed to originate).

Some Hindus practice *samadhi*, the highest level of concentrated meditation. The goal is "the complete absorption of the individual consciousness in the self at the time of death."

▶ Islam

Mohammed said we must "die before we die." Death in Islam is considered the termination of worldly life and the beginning of the afterlife. Muslims believe that death and burial marks the separation of their soul from their body to the afterlife.

What happens after death, in the afterlife, is not very clear. While Islamic tradition discusses elaborately what happens before, during, and after the moment of death, it is less descriptive about what exactly happens in the afterlife. The angel of death (in Arabic: *Malak al-Maut*) appears to arrive and take out the soul. The sinners' souls are extracted in a most painful way, while the righteous are treated gently. After the burial, two angels–*Munkar* and *Nakir*–come to question the dead in order to test their faith. The righteous believers answer correctly and live in peace and comfort in the afterlife while the sinners and disbelievers fail and punishments ensue.

Thus, every person has only one chance to prepare themselves for the life to come, where Allah will resurrect and judge every individual based on their good or bad deeds. Death is accepted as natural and merely marks a transition between the material realm and the unseen world.

> **Death is the beginning of the afterlife, but you have only one chance to prepare for it.**

▶ Christianity

Jesus taught to "give up our lives to save others" and medieval Christian monks were known to whisper in one another's ears, "Remember: you will die," so death is fundamental in Christianity.

In Christian theology, spiritual death is separation

from God. Humans are separated from God because of their sins, and are reconciled to God through the atoning sacrifice of Jesus Christ. Christians believe that because Christ defeated sin and death, those who have faith in him are made spiritually alive.

In Christianity, physical death is the separation of the soul from the body. It means the beginning of eternal life in the presence of God. According to Protestants, the unbeliever's physical death is followed by a second death (eternal death and suffering)

▶ Judaism

In Judaism, death is not considered a tragedy, but a natural process. Death, like life, has meaning and is part of God's plan. Jews believe in an afterlife, a world to come, where those who have lived a worthy life will be rewarded.

Mourning practices in Judaism are extensive, but they are not an expression of fear or distaste for death. Jewish practices relating to death and mourning have two purposes: to show respect for the dead (*kavod ha-met*), and to comfort the living (*nihum avelim*), who will miss the deceased.

When a Jewish die, their relatives say a "Kaddish" prayer. The Kaddish prayer serves to heal psychological wounds, and teach the mourner vital lessons about life and death. It is so important that it appears in the traditional service no less than 13 times and is recited at the conclusion of all the major Jewish services.

Based on Jewish laws, traditions, and customs, the dead person must be buried (not cremated) and the Jewish funeral usually takes place within one day following the death. Jewish tradition requires that a tombstone be prepared, so that the deceased will not be forgotten and the grave will not be desecrated. During the first seven days following the funeral (known as *shivaa*) the mourners generally stay at home and receive guests to help them reflect upon their loss.

▶ The spiritually inclined

The reader who is not affiliated with any prescribed religion may find that practicing death can be very fulfilling spiritually.

We are all travelers in this world; we are passing through. We came from a place that gave us life, and in a few years, or a few days, we shall move on to our next "life." We entered this world empty-handed and alone, and we shall leave empty-handed and alone. Everything we have accumulated in this life, including our very body, will be left behind. All that we can take with us from one life to the next are the imprints of the positive and negative actions we have created.

Many spiritual beings who I interviewed for this book

expressed a belief that If we ignore death, we'll miss an important opportunity to grow.

As you can see from the short summaries above, human beings have varied ways to look at and interpret death. People have witnessed death and practiced their beliefs for thousands of years. Death is unavoidable, irreversible, and therefore, humans fear it. It is understandable that a strong spiritual element has been associated with it.

Yet, the technique of practicing death is not for the sake of becoming fearful; on the contrary, it's to appreciate life and the precious time you still have.

Rather than being frightened, this practice will help you focus on the now, the people you care about, and the activities that will make your life worth living. When you are able to reflect on your death, it brings more energy to your life.

Now it's your turn:

Write below what you'll be interested to find in the afterlife, if one existed, according to your belief:

_____

_____

_____

_____

CHAPTER 8

What We Can Learn from Near-Death Experiences

"If you would, indeed, behold the spirit of death, open your heart wide unto the body of life. For life and death are one."
— Kahlil Gibran (1183–1931) Lebanese poet

You have probably heard the term "near-death experience," where someone finds themselves on the other side of life and manages to come back and tell the tale. The term near-death experience (NDE) was coined in 1975 in the book *Life After Life* by Raymond Moody.[14] Since then, many researchers have studied the phenomenon and its after effects. Apart from being fascinating stories in their own right, understanding other people's experiences can shed light on your own experience while practicing death.

An NDE is a unique experience that is reported following a near-death episode. In a near-death episode, a person is either clinically dead, near death, or in a situation where death is likely or expected. Most near-death experiencers (NDErs) have reported pleasurable experiences. These experiences commonly involve feelings of love, joy, peace, or bliss. A small percentage of NDErs have reported distressing NDEs. These experiences involve mostly feelings of terror, horror, anger, isolation, and guilt. What's interesting is that all NDErs usually report that the experience was hyper-real—even more real than earthly life.

Unfortunately, when people share their NDEs, they are often seen as "crazy" and the credibility of the experience is put into question. Nevertheless, the sheer number of testaments of NDEs from a wide range of credible individuals demonstrate that the near-death experience is not made up. Some NDErs, like the rich and famous and Hollywood stars, have nothing to gain by sharing their experience and everything to lose. Similarly, there are plenty reports of NDEs of children that are similar to adult NDEs, which is particularly interesting as children are usually not aware of the NDE phenomena and don't have religious bias. They just experience NDEs without being pre-conditioned to it.

When looking at thousands of the "classic" pleasurable reported NDEs, a pattern can be identified. The NDE includes

The reports of people who had near-death-experiences are remarkably similar. Even among little children who couldn't have read about them and weren't told about them.

four phases that tend to happen in a specific order (but can sometimes overlap).

The first phase is described as been disconnected from the physical body. You feel detached and completely peaceful, without seeing, hearing, or feeling anything in particular. You might feel a sense of freedom from pain and complete well-being.

The second phase is the naturalistic phase. NDErs say they became aware of the "natural" surroundings—typically their bodies and the surrounding area—from a perspective outside their bodies. They usually say things looked and sounded normal, aside from being unusually clear and vivid. They also often say they had unusual abilities, such as being able to see through walls and "hear" the unspoken thoughts of people nearby.

The third phase is the supernatural phase. In this phase, people reported meeting beings and environments that we usually do not consider part of the "natural" world. They may meet deceased loved ones or other non-physical entities. They say communication with these beings is "mind-to-mind" rather than spoken. Some went to beautiful environments in which objects appeared lit from within. They sometimes heard beautiful music unlike any worldly music they'd ever heard, and would move rapidly through a tunnel or void, toward a light. Upon entering the light, it was discovered the light was actually a being. Most reported feeling completely known and loved by this being. They sometimes say they experienced a "life review" where they re-viewed and re-experienced being on the receiving end of all their actions throughout life. Some say they went beyond the light, seeing cities of light and knowledge.

The fourth and final phase of the pleasurable NDE is a return to the physical body. About half of NDErs say they chose whether or not to return. When they chose to return, it was because of a relationship with one or more living people. The other half say they didn't choose to return; they either were told or made to return, or they were just suddenly "back" in their bodies.

Another interesting finding concerns NDEs and people who attempted suicide. The data[15] show that people who attempted to commit suicide are more likely to try again. Interestingly enough, people who attempted and had a near-death experience which they remember are much less likely to try again. They say they have learned that their lives have purpose—they see life as a gift. Now, when faced with hard times, they deal with the problem constructively, as all life experiences can be opportunities to deepen the ability to love and increase knowledge—a true testament of the healing ability of practicing death. (Important note: In no way do I condone suicide, and the technique described in this book advocates life, not ending it.)

> All people who had a Near Death Experience reported it as a transformational event in their life.

All NDErs have been transformed by their experience. Most came back to life because they realized that they still have a mission to accomplish or someone to help and the near-death experience helped clarify it for them and assisted them to pursue it.

They attest that they became kinder, gentler versions of the person they were before. Sometimes this change is so complete that the previous personality is no longer recognizable.

Below are five write-ups of near-death experiences which were selected from thousands of publicly available NDEs[16] as it will be more powerful if you hear the stories yourself.

Case Study: Dr. Rajiv Parti[17]

In 2008, Dr. Rajiv Parti was Chief of Anesthesiology at Bakersfield Heart Hospital. He derived his identity and happiness from the incredible wealth and prestige his job gave him. He lived in a large house, had several luxury cars, and was able to purchase almost any material good he wanted.

In August of that year, his good life changed. He was diagnosed with prostate cancer. A routine surgery eradicated the cancer but led to complications that left him in excruciating pain. He was prescribed pain medication that he soon became addicted to, and not long after, he was diagnosed with depression.

In December 2010, he went through a surgical placement of an artificial urinary sphincter. In the days after this surgery, he began running a fever of 104 to 105 degrees. Heavy antibiotics were prescribed, but he was not getting better. On Christmas Eve 2010, Dr. Parti underwent emergency surgery to drain the pelvic region of infection and remove the artificial sphincter.

It was here, on the brink of dying, that he "woke up."

Although he was under full anesthesia and totally out, he was very aware that his consciousness had separated from his body. From a vantage point near the ceiling, he said he could see the surgeon cut him, and then all of the operating room personnel react as the odor of the pus from his infected abdomen seeped into the room. He saw a nurse apply eucalyptus-scented water to everyone's surgical masks. He even heard the anesthesiologist tell a joke so dirty that he blushed when he later recalled it to the anesthesiologist in the recovery room.

Dr. Parti then left the operating room and began to drift toward familiar voices in India, where he could hear his mother and sister talking about dinner preparations. He could see they were bundled up to protect themselves from the foggy, frigid air that night.

Dr. Parti became euphoric. "People are never far away," he thought. He had the sense of his presence spreading, a feeling of oneness with the world and everyone in it. Then fear overcame him as his awareness drifted to a place where a great wildfire was raging. He could see lightning in dark clouds and smell the odor of burning meat. He realized an unseen force was pulling him into hell, leaving him "in the midst of souls who were screaming and suffering."

"What is my karma?" he wondered. "What did I do in my life or past life to deserve this punishment?"

In the middle of this horror, Dr. Parti began to have the strong awareness that the life he was living was very materialistic. It was always about him. So much so, in fact, that when he met new people Dr. Parti would ask himself: "What can I get from this person?"

The truth dawned on him there in hell: the life he was living on Earth was without love. He was not practicing forgiveness to himself or others. He also had an unsavory tendency to be harsh toward people he perceived to be lower than him in status. He felt deeply sorry for his lack of kindness, wishing he could have done certain things in his life differently. As soon as he had that realization, hell faded away.

Dr. Parti's brush with death opened an entirely new world to him—an otherworld, if you will—that replaced the materialistic world he had so carefully constructed.

Case Study: Elizabeth Taylor[18]

Elizabeth (Liz) Taylor (1932 - 2011) was a British-American actress and humanitarian who began as a child actress in the early 1940s. She officially died on the operating table while undergoing back surgery. The doctors pronounced her dead and posted a sign of her death. Five minutes later, she woke up.

As one of the most popular stars of classical Hollywood cinema in the 1950s, Taylor was interviewed by Larry King on CNN's *Larry King Live* and spoke about her NDE. She described passing through a tunnel toward a brilliant white light and encountering the spirit of Michael Todd (Taylor's third husband who was killed in a plane crash), whom she referred to as her great love. She had wanted to stay in heaven with Todd, she said, but he had told her that she had work and life ahead of her, and he *"pushed me back to my life."*

"I was pronounced dead once and actually saw the light. I find it very hard to talk about, actually, because it sounds so corny that I saw Mike. When I came to life, there were about eleven people in the room. I'd been gone for about five minutes. They had given me up for dead and put my death notice on the wall. I shared this with the people that were in the room next to me. Then after that I told another group of friends, and I thought, 'Wow, this sounds really screwy. I think I'd better keep quiet about this.'" Taylor's eleven-person medical team attested to her testimonial of the event.

In an interview with America's *AIDS* magazine,[19] Taylor described her NDE again: *"I went to that tunnel, saw the white light, and Mike. I said, 'Oh Mike, you're where I want to be.' And he said, 'No, baby. You have to turn around and go back because there is something very important for you to do. You cannot give up now.' It was Mike's strength and love that brought me back.*

"For a long time, I didn't talk about it, and it's still hard for

me to talk about. But I have shared it with people with AIDS because if the moment occurs and you're really sharing, it's real. I am not afraid of death, because I have been there."

After many years of declining health, Taylor died from congestive heart failure at the age of 79 in 2011.

Case Study: Mellen-Thomas Benedict

In 1982, I died from terminal cancer. My condition was non-operable. I chose not to have chemotherapy. I was given six to eight months to live. Before this time, I had become increasingly despondent over the ecology crisis and came to believe that nature had made a mistake – that we were probably a cancerous organism on the planet. And that is what eventually killed me.

Before my near-death experience, I tried all sorts of alternative healing methods. None helped. So I determined that this was between me and God. I had never really considered God. Neither was I into any kind of spirituality. But my approaching death sent me on a quest for more information about spirituality and alternative healing. I read various religions and philosophies. They gave hope that there was something on the other side.

I had no medical insurance, so my life savings went overnight on tests. Unwilling to drag my family into this, I determined to handle this myself. I ended up in hospice care and was blessed with an angel for my hospice caretaker, whom I will call Anne. She stayed with me through all that was to follow.

One night I woke up at 4:30AM and I knew that this was it. I was going to die. I called a few friends and said good-bye. I woke up Anne and made her promise that my dead body would remain undisturbed for six hours, since I had read that all kinds of interesting things happen when you die. I went back to sleep. The next thing I remember, I was fully aware and standing up. Yet my body was lying in the bed. I seemed to be surrounded by darkness, yet I could see every room in the house, and the roof, and even under the house.

A Light shone. I turned toward it, and was aware of its similarity to what others have described in near-death experiences. It was magnificent and tangible, alluring. I wanted to go toward that Light like I might want to go into my ideal mother's or father's arms. As I moved toward the Light, I knew that if I went into the Light, I would be dead. So I said/felt, "Please wait. I would like to talk to you before I go."

The entire experience halted. I discovered that I was in control of the experience. My request was honored. I had conversations with the Light. That's the best way I can describe it. The Light changed into different figures, like Jesus, Buddha, Krishna, archetypal images and signs.

It was the most beautiful thing I have ever seen. It was like all the love you've ever wanted, and it was the kind of love that cures, heals, regenerates. I was ready to go at that time. I said, "I am ready, take me." Then the Light turned into the most beautiful thing that I have ever seen: a mandala of human souls on this planet. I saw that we are the most beautiful creations–elegant, exotic . . . everything.

I just cannot say enough about how it changed my opinion of human beings in an instant. I said/thought/felt, "Oh, God, I didn't realize." I was astonished to find that there was no evil in any soul. People may do terrible things out of ignorance and lack, but no soul is evil. "What all people seek–what sustains them–is love," the Light told me. "What distorts people is a lack of love."

I thanked the Light of God with all my heart. The best thing I could come up with was: "Oh dear God, dear Universe, dear Great Self, I love my Life." The Light seemed to breathe me in even more deeply, absorbing me. I entered into another realm more profound than the last, and was aware of an enormous stream of Light, vast and full, deep. I asked what it was. The Light answered, "This is the River of Life.

*Drink of this manna water to your heart's content."
I drank deeply, in ecstasy.*

Suddenly I seemed to be rocketing away from the planet on this stream of Life. I saw the earth fly away. The solar system whizzed by and disappeared. I flew through the center of the galaxy, absorbing more knowledge as I went. I learned that this galaxy – and the entire Universe – is bursting with many different varieties of life. I saw many worlds. We are not alone in this Universe. It seemed as if all the creations in the Universe soared past me and vanished in a speck of Light.

Then a second Light appeared. As I passed into the second Light, I could perceive forever, beyond Infinity. I was in the Void, pre-Creation, the beginning of time, the first Word or vibration. I rested in the Eye of Creation and it seemed that I touched the Face of God. It was not a religious feeling. I was simply at One with Absolute Life and Consciousness.

I rode the stream directly into the center of the Light. I felt embraced by the Light as it took me in with its breath again. And the truth was obvious that there is no death; that nothing is born and nothing dies; that we are immortal beings, part of a natural living system that recycles itself endlessly.

It would take me years to assimilate the Void experience. It was less than nothing, yet greater than anything. Creation is God exploring God's Self through every way imaginable. Through every piece of hair on your head, through every leaf on every tree, through every atom. God is exploring God's Self. I saw everything as the Self of all. God is here. That's what it is all about. Everything is made of light; everything is alive.

I was never told that I had to come back. I just knew that I would. It was only natural, from what I had seen. As I began my return to the life cycle, it never crossed my mind, nor was I told, that I would return to the same body. It did not matter. I had complete trust in the Light and the Life process.

As the stream merged with the great Light, I asked never to forget the revelations and the feelings of what I had learned on the other side. I thought of myself as a human again and I was happy to be that. From what I have seen, I would be happy to be an atom in this universe. An atom. So to be the human part of God . . . this is the most fantastic blessing. For each and every one of us to be the human part of this experience is awesome, and magnificent. Each and every one of us, no matter where we are, screwed up or not, is a blessing to the planet, right where we are. So I went through the reincarnation process expecting to be a baby somewhere.

But I reincarnated back into this body. I was so

surprised when I opened my eyes, to be back in this body, back in my room with someone looking over me, crying her eyes out. It was Anne, my hospice caretaker. She had found me dead thirty minutes before. We do not know how long I was dead, only that she found me thirty minutes before. She had honored my wish to have my newly-dead body left alone. She can verify that I really was dead.

It was not a near-death experience. I believe I probably experienced death itself for at least an hour and a half. When I later awakened and saw the light outside, confused, I tried to get up to go to it, but I fell out of the bed. She heard a loud "clunk," ran in, and found me on the floor. When I recovered, I was surprised and awed about what had happened. I had no memory at first of the experience. I kept slipping out of this world and kept asking, "Am I alive?" This world seemed more like a dream than that one.

Within three days, I was feeling normal again, clearer, yet different than ever before. My memories of the journey came back later. But from my return I could find nothing wrong with any human being I had ever seen. Previous to my death I was judgmental, believing that people were really screwed up.

About three months later a friend said I should get tested for the cancer. So I got the scans and so forth. I felt healthy. I still remember the doctor at the clinic looking at the "before" and "after" scans. He said, "I can find no sign of cancer now." "A miracle?" I asked. "No," he answered. "These things happen . . . . spontaneous remission." He seemed unimpressed. But I was impressed. I knew it was a miracle.

I went over to the other side with a lot of fears about toxic waste, nuclear missiles, the population explosion, the rain forest. I came back loving every single problem. Knowing that maybe we can blow up the planet, we finally realize that maybe we are all here together. For a period, they had to keep setting off more bombs to get it into us. Then we started saying, "We do not need this anymore." Now we are actually in a safer world than we have ever been in, and it is going to get even safer.

Earth is in the process of domesticating itself, and we are cells on that Body. Population increase is getting very close to the optimal range of energy to cause a shift in consciousness. That shift in consciousness will change politics, money, energy, and more.

Since my return I have experienced the Light spontaneously. I have learned how to get to that space in my meditation. You can also do this. You don't have to die first. You are wired for it already. The body is the most magnificent Light being there is.

Note: The above text is a concise, slightly edited summary.[20]

Case Study: Cecile (11 years old)

Cecile and her younger brother went swimming in the river when they both began to drown. Only Cecile survived to tell her near-death experience:

> *My brother and I went swimming. He had a problem. I tried to get him out of the water, but in his panic he pulled me under several times. We both drowned. He died and I came back. I can remember it all like yesterday. Just as I could no longer stay afloat, a strange sound like ringing in my ears started. A peaceful feeling came over me. I felt my spirit come out of my body and I went into a black void. That was a little frightening.*
>
> *A long way off there was a pinprick of light. I moved toward it, slowly at first, then faster and faster as if I were on top of a train accelerating. Then I stopped and stepped fully into the light. I noticed everything—sky, buildings, glass—emitted its own light and everything was much more colorful than what we see here. A river meandered. On the other side was a city, and a road running through it to another city, and another city and another and another.*
>
> *Right in front of me but across the river were three men. They projected themselves to me. They didn't*

walk or fly; they projected over. I didn't recognize them, yet I knew one was Lynn Bibb. (I was named after him. He died a matter of weeks before I was born.) I knew these three men were looking out for me, like a welcoming committee to escort me over the river to the first city. I had the feeling that if I went with them, there would be no coming back, so I hesitated.

The first city was like first grade. People stayed there until they were ready to go to the next city—your eternal progression, from city to city. Behind me and to the left was a strong light source, very brilliant and filled with love. I knew it was a person. I called it God for lack of a better term. I could not see it; I felt what seemed like a male presence. He communicated to me, not so much in words but telepathically, and he asked, "Why did you hesitate?"

I replied, "Well, I'm kind of young to die." He chuckled. "We have babies die."

I said, "There's some things I want to know first." He replied, "What do you want to know?"

We walked as I asked about the universe and reasons for everything. All of these things were shown to me. Then he wondered if I still wanted to return to the physical world.

"I do want to return."

He asked, "Why?"

> *I said I would help my mother whom my father had left with four children and one on the way. God kind of chuckled and asked me for the real reason. I said I would leave the earth a little better than I found it.*
>
> *"Then you may return with some of the knowledge of the things you have learned, but the rest will be veiled for a time. Live in such a way that you will not be going back when you return here again."*
>
> *I woke up face down in the mud of the river bottom and was 'lifted' to the top. I threw up great amounts of water, then pulled myself out of the river only to discover my brother had died.*

Note: The above text is a concise, slightly edited summary.[21]

Case Study: Dr. Dianne Morrissey

When Dr. Dianne Morrissey (1949-2009) was twenty-eight years old, she was electrocuted and had a very profound near-death experience. Her experience transformed her entire life in a very big way:

> *I bent over to pick up the plastic tubing. As I began to straighten up, I accidentally bumped the tubing on the edge of the tank. My body was thrown backward and to one side by the electrical current. My body crashed to the floor, thrown with such force that my head went right through the drywall, about a foot above the floor. I never felt the injuries, however,*

because I was no longer in my body. I was actually watching my electrocution from above!

As my body bent over in shock, I had the most uncanny knowledge that death was ahead of me. I began to mourn the loss of everything I'd known: the earth, my home, my friends—all that I'd been aware of, all that I loved. Everything I'd believed to be true and lasting was slipping away from me. I was face-to-face with death, face-to-face with the unknown.

"How could I be out of my body and still be alive?" I wondered, astonished.

Suddenly, I was aware that I was inside a vast, seemingly infinite blackness. I wasn't sure where this blackness was in relationship to the earth, but for some reason I was unafraid. My blackout period was brief, for I now found myself back in my home, but in a new form. I was transparent, yet I still looked like me.

How elated I felt! Now, out of my body, I had no worries, no cares. Never had I felt like this when I was "alive." My entire spirit body was transparent, and I was inside a glowing white light that extended about three feet around me. At that moment, an awareness overtook me—I am not my physical body! This realization made me feel so free, so wonderful! My spirit was glowing with a white light that illuminated the entire room.

Then, I was up near the ceiling again. Everything still looked the same—the furnishings, the walls—but there was a new awareness about the dimension to the scene—it had become transparent. I could see everything more clearly than ever before, and like a scientist, I found myself looking at life through a microscope, discovering minuscule particles of matter normally invisible.

Now, I saw that everything was shrouded by a mist. Despite a lack of gravity, I could easily control my direction, and when I moved into the living room, I noticed that I had just walked through the glass coffee table. "Wow! How did I do that?" I marveled.

Tuffy my dog suddenly entered the den and began nipping at my face and pawing at my arm, trying to get my body to wake up. I knew that his relentless attempts to awaken my physical body wouldn't work, yet I was proud of him for trying, and even hoped his efforts might work. I wondered where his chum, Penny, was, and suddenly I was next to her in the backyard. I opened my mouth to talk to her and felt my tongue moving, but no sounds came out. I could distinctly hear my voice, and then realized it was coming from my mind. I tried several times to get Penny's attention, yelling, "Penny, can you see me? Penny, can you hear me?" Apparently, she didn't, because there was no response.

Next, I walked around my backyard. As I looked through the walls of my house toward the front sidewalk, I noticed a man walking down the street. Eagerly, I flew to him, right through the walls, and tried to get his attention. Staring deeply into his eyes, I said forcefully, "Can you help me? I need help." Then I tried to shake his shoulders, but he still didn't notice me. Frustrated, I tried to touch his shoulder to get him to look at me, and my hand went through his upper right shoulder blade and out his back. This startled me.

"What am I to do?" I wondered, becoming upset when I realized that the man could neither see nor hear me. Instantly, I was back in my yard again, Penny beside me. I noticed that whenever I felt any apprehension, I was instantly moved to a place of greater comfort.

On the way back to the den, I stopped right in the middle of the wall between rooms. I sensed that I was to look down at something fantastic, and as I gazed downward, as soon as I saw that the silver cord was attached to my physical body, my spirit body was thrust into a dark tunnel. I moved through it with great speed, traveling faster than I could have imagined possible. Although the tunnel was filled with an all-consuming darkness, I felt peaceful and unafraid.

I was met by a radiant angelic female being who stood before me, smiling. As she moved toward me, I walked to meet her. Her love surrounded me, and my spirit was filled with an almost unbearable joy.

She walked closer and stood with me; then, we were both lifted about ten inches into the air, as if we were on a platform moving upward. Extending her arm before her, she indicated that I was to look to my left. As I turned my eyes left, the entire scene changed into a life review, a vivid, three-dimensional color display of my entire life. Every detail of every second, every feeling, every thought while I had been alive on Earth was displayed before me in perfect chronological order, from my birth until my electrocution.

I was re-living my entire twenty-eight years simultaneously! The best experiences brought me feelings of great joy. I felt as if every spirit in Heaven was watching with me, applauding me, and letting me know that God approved of my caring, unselfish deeds. I will never forget the love that surrounded me at that moment, or the joy that ran through me. Can you imagine being hugged by God and your angel? It's an experience that defies description!

It was then that I asked myself, Am I dead? Am I really dead?

Finally, my life review was finished, and I was whisked away from the angelic being and returned to the tunnel. This time, I seemed to be falling through it, finally emerging in another room, in another dimension. It was a world far more beautiful than any I could ever have imagined, a place of awesome serenity. The peace and calm I felt surpassed any previous notions I had had about Heaven, and I knew, in the deepest part of my soul, that God was here.

In this rapturous place, I recognized that there were two aspects of "me." My soul was my consciousness, everything that had made me who I had been and what I had become. My spirit, on the other hand, was the part of me that was now transparent and glowing, dressed in white.

Do you remember how it felt, long ago, to be held and rocked in your mother's loving arms? Take this to the hundredth power and you're still light years away from the feeling of total peace and comfort that surrounded me. I felt the love of every mother in the universe being poured inside me for now and for all eternity. At that moment, I knew that nothing ever dies. Nothing ever dies!

Then, I sensed that I must look to my right, through the lace. There, I could see a pinpoint of Light coming from the next room, the pinpoint of Light became a brilliant white beam a trillion times brighter than the brightest sun imaginable, and began to move toward me. At first, it appeared to be bands of multifaceted light being stretched and pulled together.

I was awestruck, overwhelmed by the Light, the love, the love of God for me! I knew I could go into this Light, which was part of a tremendous force. And, although the Light was brighter than a thousand suns, it didn't hurt my eyes.

I was going to have to choose between staying in the Light and going back to Earth. Somehow, I knew that if I went into the next room, into the Light, I could never return to my body. I felt torn between two desires: wanting to go into the Light, and wanting to touch something tangible and retain my connection with all that was physical. Both desires grew stronger. The Light became more intense, more radiant, more loving. As I lifted the lace and extended my hand toward the brilliance, wanting to touch the Light, it rushed under the lace and touched the outstretched middle finger of my right hand.

As soon as the Light touched me, I was transformed. The Light and my spirit merged—I had entered the Light of God, and all sense of my spirit body was gone. My consciousness, fully alive, was now totally connected to God. Within the Light, I knew that everyone and everything is connected to it. God is in everyone, always and forever. Within the Light was the cure for all diseases; within the Light was all the knowledge of every planet, every galaxy, every universe. Indeed, the Light was Wisdom and Love beyond all comprehension.

This Light and my spirit mingled for what felt like an eternity, but eventually I began to sense with great urgency that the time had come to choose whether I would stay here or return to physical life. How could I decide?

Suddenly, my spirit body was back in the tunnel. The angelic being was waiting for me. She looked at me and asked telepathically, "What do you want, Dianne?"

I said, "I want to go into the Light, and I want to touch things."

I was suddenly thrust forward through the tunnel, and when I looked down, I was aghast to see my physical body below me. I thought, How sad; she has done so very little. *I realized "Dianne" hadn't touched as many people as she could have while alive. And I realized how life could be enriched by touching others' lives more deeply and meaningfully.*

While alive, as Dianne, I had always known that my life was full of certain pleasures: a beautiful home, a good job, a nice car, warm friends, a wonderful family, a beloved best friend, and a musical career I loved. But none of these matter anymore, *I thought, reversing myself again.* Only the Light mattered. *To my surprise, I began to feel a persistent pulling sensation from about four inches above my navel. I tried to resist it, for I sensed a new process was beginning, one that might take me from this place, from God. I didn't want to leave behind such feelings of elation. Yes, I wanted to touch things, but I wanted the Light even more.*

Suddenly, I was rushing through the tunnel again. When I emerged, I was up near the ceiling in the den, looking down at my physical body below me. Then, without warning, I was thrust swiftly back into my body, entering through the back of my neck, with my spirit legs and arms together, like a diver doing a jackknife.

As I re-entered my body, I knew that the God within me could never die, and I knew that I could never die. For a moment, I actually saw myself half in and half out of my body. Then, with a jolt, I landed fully back in my body.

Oh, my God, *I thought,* how could I have chosen to come back? I want to be in the Light again. *Tears ran down my cheeks and I wept, desolate about the choice that had been made. Had it really been my choice? I couldn't believe that I had decided to come back.*

I now believe that one reason I was sent back was

to help people feel better about dying—and to learn that death is not an end, but a new beginning.

Note: The above text is a concise, slightly edited summary.[22]

CHAPTER 9

Final Thoughts

"Spoiler alert: Life's a movie where everyone dies at the end."

—Lizzy Miles

We rarely think about our death, let alone try to truly understand the event we will all experience one day. The cliché "Live every day as though it's your last" looks nice on a bumper sticker but is unhelpful advice to most of us, especially when deep down, we know that today is probably not our last day (you have years of experience proving it).

People who drank deep from the fountain of wisdom, such as Mozart, called death "the key to unlocking the door to true happiness." Shakespeare wrote, "When we are prepared for death, life is sweeter." Plato, on his deathbed, was asked to summarize his life's work. Coming out of a daydream, he said simply, "Practice dying."

I'm not sure what I'd do if I was going to die tomorrow—maybe round up all my loved ones and fly them to meet for a fun last day in Hawaii? Or maybe just throw an intimate dinner with my best friends, the kind where everyone ends up pleasantly buzzed, not just from the booze and good food but all the laughs and stories told around a bonfire on the beach?

Either way, between now and that last day, I'll be working hard to make sure that I'm spending time and energy on the things that are really important to me, which I continue to uncover through my death-practice.

While my sister's cancer was initially devastating news to our family, we grew stronger from her near-death experience, realizing our insignificance, and re-focused our energy on the things that were truly important to us.

I can honestly say that by confronting death and practicing it, I now live a more complete, holistic, and happier life.

It is my hope that you will find the same as you embark on this transformative journey to practice death and distill the essence of your life into what is most important to you.

Live well.

APPENDIX A

Questions and Answers

"I hate to be the bearer of bad news but you're gonna die!"

—Captain James Kirk, Star Trek commander

Since I started running workshops on the benefits of practicing death, I've received many questions, some personal (which will not be covered in this appendix) and some general, about the practice.

I've included several questions and answers that might be valuable to you in your practice:

> A: Question: Every time I enter into the death experience, I get very emotional and start crying, Is it normal?

> A: Answer: Yes, this is very normal and nothing to be concerned about. The simulation of your parting moments is a very emotionally-charged event which might raise feelings of fear, exhilaration, and relief—sometimes all at the same time. Tears are a normal expression of heightened feelings. Therefore, let the

tears come and don't try to suppress and hold them in. Let yourself be fully immersed in the experience.

B: Question: I've been practicing death for three months now and love it as it is helping me live a healthier life, something I struggled with for years. I want my husband to try it too, as it could be very helpful for him, but he's resistant to the idea. What can I do to convince him?

B: Answer: There is an old saying, "You can drag a horse to the water, but you can't force it to drink." Different people have different feelings regarding their own death. Your husband might not be open or ready to experience it just yet. The best way is to help him understand the value and the benefits of the practice. Let him realize, with your help, the positive transformation you experienced and, hopefully, this will pique his interest, too.

C: Question: I've been married to my husband for forty-two years and our greatest fear is not of dying, but living without each other. Do you have a special practice for couples?

C: Answer: To similar couples who attend my workshops, I advise to go through the practice together. Lay down side-by-side, holding one of your partner's hands. It allows each person to have his own individual experience while at the same time being attuned to the energy and emotions of their partner (and potentially incorporating it in their own experience). The feedback I've received from couples who have been living with each other for years and were doing the exercise together is quite amazing. In most cases, they can "see" and feel a similar experience, describing the same location and individuals surrounding them on their death bed. It is a great way to fulfil the promise, some say, "Till death do us part."

D: Question: I was practicing death for once a week for the first month after the workshop, but at some point I started skipping the practice and now I stopped. It was helpful while I was doing it. Any advice on how to be more consistent with it?

D: Answer: A habit is usually created after we incorporate the activity into our routine for sixty days. The ten minutes, once a week, practice was designed to be conducted in the comfort of the practitioner's home. This is a short time investment considering the transformational benefits it provides. To my workshop attendees, I recommend picking a specific day of the week and scheduling the practice on your calendar as the first activity in your morning that day. This way, nothing should prevent you from achieving it. Normally, once practitioners completed eight weekly practices, they swear by it and find that they are looking forward to their next practice–as at this point their habit was formed and they find it easy to keep the practice and enjoy its benefits.

E: Question: Ranan, I love the concept of practicing death and it makes a lot of sense to me. Unfortunately, when I try to implement it while lying in the bed in the morning, as you suggested, I tend to fall asleep and very rarely remember my experience. Any ideas on what should I do?

E: Answer: You describe a common phenomenon, especially for individuals who go to sleep late and wake up early. Your body might be sleep-deprived and, therefore, takes advantage of the time in which you lay down calmly to catch few more precious minutes of sleep. I suggest you try to go to sleep earlier in the night prior to your practice and test if the added sleep helped you avoid falling asleep during the death practice. At the end of the day, remembering and acting upon what you have experienced during the death simulation will drive the positive transformation in your life. You can experiment with different times to go to bed to make sure your body gets the sleep it needs.

F: Question: My wife and I attended your talk and liked it a lot. Since we started practicing, we both went through a series of realizations that made us change priorities. We were thinking that it would be nice to have a community of practitioners who could share their experiences. Can you point us to where we could connect with such group?

F: Answer: We usually create a dedicated group for attendees of each workshop, as participants get to know each other and share personal experiences.

You can join the group of like-minded death practitioners and read about other practitioners' experiences and transformations and also share your experience at the Facebook group Practice Death located at https://www.facebook.com/groups/790387561318067/

APPENDIX B

References

1. Bronnie Ware, *The Top Five Regrets of the Dying: A Life Transformed by the Dearly Departing*, Hay House, Mar 20, 2012.
2. Randy Pausch, *The Last Lecture*, Hyperion; 1st edition (April 8, 2008).
3. https://www.comresglobal.com/wp-content/themes/comres/poll/Dying_matters_16_May_2011.pdf.
4. Ernest Becker, *The Denial of Death*, Free Press, May 8, 1997.
5. Amelia Goranson, Ryan S. Ritter, Adam Waytz, Michael I. Norton, Kurt Gray, *Dying is Unexpectedly Positive*, Psychological Science, vol. 28, 7: pp. 988-999. , First Published June 1, 2017.
6. http://time.com/5159892/how-to-become-less-afraid-of-death/.
7. Carstensen LL, Isaacowitz DM, Charles ST, *Taking time seriously. A theory of socioemotional selectivity.* American Psychology, 54(3):165-81, March 1999.
8. Karen Kangas Dwyer, Marlina M. Davidson, *Is Public Speaking Really More Feared Than Death?*, Communication Research Reports 29(2):99-107, April 2012.

9. Stephen R. Covey, *The 7 Habits of Highly Effective People: Powerful Lessons in Personal Change*, Simon & Schuster; Anniversary edition, November 19, 2013.
10. https://www.forbes.com/sites/carmine-gallo/2011/11/11/your-emotionally-disconnected-employees/#13bcec4e42d5.
11. Matthew T. Gailliot, Tyler F. Stillman, Brandon J. Schmeichel, Jon K. Maner and E. Ashby Plant M, *Mortality Salience Increases Adherence to Salient Norms and Values*, Society Psychology, Bull 2008 34: 993.
12. Lati Rinbochay & Jeffrey Hopkins, *Death, Intermediate State and Rebirth in Tibetan Buddhism*, Snow Lion Publications, 1985.
13. *The Tibetan Book of the Dead*, Penguin publishing, January 30, 2007.
14. Raymond Moody, *Life After Life*, HarperOne, September 8, 2015.
15. Robert Carroll, Chris Metcalfe, David Gunnell, Hospital Presenting Self-Harm and Risk of Fatal and Non-Fatal Repetition: Systematic Review and Meta-Analysis, Pone, February 28, 2014.
16. https://www.near-death.com/.
17. Rajiv Parti M.D and Raymood Moody, *Dying to Wake Up: A Doctor's Voyage into the Afterlife and the Wisdom He Brought Back*, Atria Books, August 15, 2017.
18. https://www.near-death.com/experiences/rich-and-famous.html#a04.

19. A&U Magazine, America's AIDS Magazine, February 2003 issue.
20. Https://www.near-death.com/reincarnation/experiences/mellen-thomas-benedict.html.
21. https://www.near-death.com/experiences/children.html.
22. https://www.near-death.com/experiences/notable/dianne-morrissey.html.

Other recommended reading:

Stephen Levine, *Who Dies?: An Investigation of Conscious Living and Conscious Dying*, Anchor, January 18, 1989

Rodney Smith, *Lessons from the Dying*, Rodney Smith, Wisdom Publications, January 30, 2012

Elisabeth Kubler Rose, *On Life After Death*, CelestialArts, 1991

The Tibetan Book of the Dead, Penguin Publishing, January 30, 2007

Stephen Levine, *A Year to Live: How to Live This Year as If It Were Your Last*, Publisher: Harmony, April 14 1998

Bronnie Ware, *The Top Five Regrets of the Dying: A Life Transformed by the Dearly Departing*, Hay House Inc., March 20, 2012

https://www.theatlantic.com/health/archive/2015/05/what-good-is-thinking-about-death/394151/

https://www.theatlantic.com/health/archive/2013/10/death-is-having-a-moment/280777/

https://www.theatlantic.com/health/archive/2012/05/how-the-unrelenting-threat-of-death-shapes-our-behavior/256728/

https://www.nytimes.com/2016/01/10/opinion/sunday/to-be-happier-start-thinking-more-about-your-death.html

https://www.psychologytoday.com/au/blog/passion/201602/the-5-benefits-mortality-meditation-part-1

www.ingramcontent.com/pod-product-compliance
Lightning Source LLC
LaVergne TN
LVHW011425080426
835512LV00005B/268